Moral Stories

The Hidden Treasure

Om KIDZ
An imprint of Om Books International

An old man lived in a village. He had four sons. None of them was as hardworking as their father. They wasted their time in idle pursuits. This worried the old man.

One day, the old man fell seriously ill and he was soon counting his last days on Earth. *I am really worried about my sons,* the old man thought to himself as he lay on his deathbed.

How will they survive after I'm gone? They do not want to do any kind of work.

The old man had tried to change his sons' behaviour many times. He did this again as his health deteriorated. "Nothing is more rewarding than hard work, my sons!" the old man told them.

His sons were under the impression that Lady Luck would smile on them one day and they would become rich beyond their wildest dreams. There was no need for them to work as hard as their father. Hence they paid no heed to their father's advice.

The old man realised that there was no other option but to play a trick on his sons so that they would understand the importance of hard work.

One day, he called his sons over to his room and said, “My sons, I am leaving behind a treasure box for you. Ensure that you share the contents of the treasure box equally, so that all of you lead a happy life after I am gone.”

"What is in the treasure box, father?" the sons asked the old man happily.

"Gold coins and precious gems!" the old man replied.

"Where is the treasure box?" the sons asked.

"Well, I can't remember that," the old man replied. "I do remember that I had buried it somewhere on our land, so that it was hidden from robbers. But I do not recall the exact place where it is buried. You must find it!" he urged his sons.

The lazy sons were happy to hear about the treasure box buried on their land but at the same time, they were disappointed that their father had forgotten where it was buried. A few days later, the old man passed away.

“Let us find the treasure without wasting any more time,” the sons decided.

They dug their entire land and worked harder than ever to look for the treasure. Despite all their efforts, they failed to discover any treasure.

The sons believed that the treasure must be buried at a specific spot where their father used to rest on their land. So, they decided to concentrate all their energies on that particular spot and dig there. The particular spot did not have the treasure box but as the sons dug deep, they found a water source.

The other farmers rushed to the spot on seeing water flow out. They informed the four sons about the positives of finding water on land and showed them ways of farming the land.

The four sons then sowed vegetable and grain seeds on the land. The steady supply of water had made the land very fertile and soon, it yielded crops aplenty. The sons sold their produce in the market and made a great deal of money.

"Hard work was what our father had actually meant by the 'treasure box'," the eldest son told his brothers as they finally realised what their father had been trying to say. The four brothers worked hard from then on and went on to live happy and prosperous lives!